Dedicated to
My parents,
for raising me to believe that
anything was possible.
And to my Love,
for making everything possible.

SHABNAM SIRAJ

Love & Lavender

AL-LINA
PUBLICATION

Write with passion...
We are here for your dreams...

Published by
AL – LINA PUBLICATION
Chennai, India
Email : linapublication@gmail.com

First Edition || July 2024

ISBN 9789394702547

Cover design & Book formatting by
AL – LINA PUBLICATION and Team

Contents

Love And Lavender

A girl from small town name as a Clara. Clara was very Independent and courageous. Her eyes are like pools of liquid amber, reflecting both wisdom and innocence. Long strands of chestnut hair cascaded down her slender frame, catching the sunlight in a mesmerizing dance of golden hues.

Her smile, a beacon of warmth and sincerity, could illuminate the darkest corners of any soul, radiating a gentle charm that drew others in with effortless grace.

Her overall demeanor exuded a quiet confidence, a subtle blend of resilience and vulnerability. With every step, she carried herself with poise, a testament to her inner strength and unwavering resolve. Yet beneath the surface, there lingered a delicate vulnerability that spoke of the depth of her heart and the richness of her spirit.

In her presence, one couldn't help but be captivated by the captivating mystery of her essence, a tapestry woven with threads of grace, elegance, and quiet intensity.

Clara didn't understand the meaning of Love; she believed only in fairy tales. She had no interest in love and affection. She was very happy in her life.

One day, such a thing happened that her life changed.

This is a story of those days when she was merely 17'. Clara and her parents visited to their cousin's house for the first time, over there was a young gentle man who had fallen in love with Clara. She didn't even know that someone would be so enamored with her, that someone would desire her so passionately.

The name of a young man was Jack. At that moment, the boy had fervently prayed from his heart, wishing that she would become his life time partner, how wonderful it would be. Jack was stunned by Clara's beauty, which captivated him completely. Jack was of a very Shy disposition, and he had never experienced love for any girl before, **but upon seeing Clara for the first time, he fell in Love.**

After a while, they departed. On that day, Clara had given a present to Jack's mom, a wall clock. Jack accepted the gift with great affection and kept it carefully. That Token was very precious for jack because it was given by Clara.

Due to his shy demeanor, Jack couldn't establish contact with Clara. He was eagerly anticipating the next opportunity to meet her again and wondering when their next encounter would take place.

One day, Jack's heart skipped a beat when he encountered Clara again at Jack's cousin's wedding. Jack was taken aback. He realized that he shouldn't let this opportunity slip away, as there might not be another chance for them to meet. He made numerous attempts to establish contact with Clara, but unfortunately, it still wasn't possible at that time. Eventually by coincidence, he found a means to reach out to Clara.

Jack was overwhelmed with happiness; he felt as though he had discovered the essence of worldly joy simply by acquiring a way to reach out to her. Clara was engrossed in her thoughts when suddenly a message beeped.

And the message was "Hey, beautiful girl could you spare some valuable time to chat?"

The girl replied, "who are you? And why should I talk to you? I don't talk to strangers; there's no reason for me to talk to you".

Jack began to contemplate what to say and how to request Clara to talk. He asked her, "can we be Allies?" However Clara declined and blocked jack. Jack tried very hard, but Clara wasn't interested in talking to strangers.

Jack didn't give up because how could he?

IT WAS LOVE AT FIRST SIGHT.

One day, after numerous attempts, Clara finally agreed to talk to Jack, although she behaved very rudely towards him. Even in that situation, Jack was brimming with happiness.

Jack possessed an exceptional personality; he was a remarkably talented young man, smart and dashing. He had a plethora of admirable qualities.

A conversation between Clara and Jack began, and days passed. Initially, Clara wasn't very interested in talking, but Jack always yearned to communicate with Clara. He would constantly find excuses just to have a conversation with her. Clara used to be busy with her schedule, unable to allocate proper time, but over time, conversations started deepening and they grew closer. Clara randomly asked Jack what he wanted in life, what his goal was. Jack smiled and said, "I just want you. My only goal is to have you and to see you succeed in life."

The girl said, "what nonsense are you talking?". He replied, "no, these are not rubbish talks. Since I've seen you, I haven't seen anything else."

"Will you be my valentine forever?" That's how Jack proposed to Clara.

Clara rejected by saying that she doesn't like all these talks about love and affection. She wants to achieve a lot in her life, and her parents wouldn't approve of their love either. Actually, even today, in some households, girls are not allowed to marry according to their choices. Jack's heart broke; he was very upset after hearing Clara's response.

Jack didn't lose hope. He said, "Okay, we'll just be best friends," but then they became close again.

Jack shared his feelings with Clara, "I love you deeply. Will you be my companion? I'll convince everyone for you, even my parents. I'll handle them."

Clara once again expressed the heartbreaking statement that it's not possible, saying, "Sorry, I'm not interested. I only see you as a friend. I love you as a friend."

Clara used to have a friend named Lily, who was always by her side. Lily was very kind-hearted, and Clara shared all her secrets with her, and vice versa. One morning, when Lily came over, only Clara was present at home as her parents were out. Clara was sitting quietly, and when asked what was bothering her, she shared the secret that Jack had proposed to her, but she hadn't accepted. Lily suggested that she should have accepted if he was good. Clara's decision upset Lily, yet she advised Clara to take more time and make the right decision.

Clara believed that a Prince Charming would come for her; she solely believed in the imaginary world. Many proposals came her way, but she kept rejecting them. Jack, however, never stopped trying; he must have proposed more than 15 times, but his heart would break every time. Gradually, he learned to lose courage. Now, she wasn't talking about those conversations anymore, and slowly, distances grew between them.

Jack came to the realization that Clara's standards were high, and perhaps his love would never succeed. He began to believe that Clara would never understand the state of his heart.

Both were busy and content in their respective lives for some time. One evening, something happened that changed their lives drastically. Despite seeming impossible, a stormy weather brewed suddenly with strong winds blowing. In the midst of this, Clara's message came unexpectedly to Jack, leaving him bewildered, wondering if he was dreaming. However, it was indeed true. They began conversing, and Jack couldn't fathom the reason behind Clara's message.

Eventually, Clara proposed to Jack amidst their conversation, asking, "Will you be my valentine?" Jack was overwhelmed, momentarily unable to comprehend, appearing deeply shocked, as this was not a usual occurrence. Clara awaited his reply anxiously. Jack, puzzled, questioned why she wasn't ready to spend her life with him before, and how and why the sudden change. Clara responded that she had been restless for some time, with thoughts of him occupying her mind.

She realized she should have accepted his proposal and confessed her newfound love for him. "I'm really sorry I couldn't understand you.

Now I am in love with you. I feel for you," she expressed. This was exactly what Jack had hoped for, so he replied with a resounding "yes." In the following days, they grew closer. Jack had never imagined in his dreams that Clara would say yes to his proposal.

That day became the best day of their lives, and slowly their bond grew stronger. They started having very sweet conversations with each other. They became very close to each other. It was a long-distance relationship for both of them, and they missed each other a lot.

After some time, a day came when Jack said to Clara, "I want to meet you. Will you give me some of your precious time?"

Clara was surprised and troubled upon hearing this, and now she started thinking about how she would meet him. Because Clara was afraid of her parents, she said, "Sorry, this is not possible."

Jack asked, "Why is this not possible? If you say, I can make every impossible thing possible for you."

Clara replied, "My parents cling to old beliefs, they will never allow this to happen." Jack responded, "My love, leave everything to me, I can handle it all." With earnest pleading, Jack said, "Please, dear, just grant us one glimpse of each other."

After hearing so much pleading, Clara finally agreed to meet Jack. Jack said, "I will wait for you at Ferrnhills Palace." Clara replied, "Okay, I will come."

Both were restless to meet each other. It was the season of love, the rain started pouring heavily, there was the sound of thunder, both were lost in each other's thoughts, waiting for that moment. The night passed like this. In the joy of meeting, both of their sleep seemed to disappear. Now, as much as there was happiness, there was also fear.

Morning arrived, the weather was pleasant, the chirping of birds could be heard, the alarm started ringing. Jack woke up. Checking the time, it was 5:30 in the morning. He quickly got up, freshened up, put on his suit, wore his watch, shoes, and socks. Jack's excitement to meet increased, but he also felt shy about the first meeting.

Now, he started thinking about being ready to meet her, but then the thought came of what gift to get for Clara. Immediately, he went to a good showroom and bought a gold chain and a large bouquet of roses. Because he had heard from someone that Clara really likes roses... Now Jack is completely ready.

Clara was almost ready too, she had also worn a white oversized gown, she had then put on a white pearl necklace, earrings, and a ring. She had bought a nice wristwatch for Jack from a very big showroom..

Finally, the time had come to meet.

Jack had crossed the ocean just to catch a glimpse of Clara.

Jack had arranged the magnificent palace especially for Clara, which was adorned with candles, illuminating the place.

Now Clara had arrived there to meet Jack, as soon as she entered, it started raining flowers on her. Clara was utterly shocked.

The lights dimmed on their own and all the candles started glowing, the gentle strumming of guitars could be heard, Jack had arranged a very romantic date for Clara. Clara couldn't understand anything, she just stood there, slowly she heard someone walking, she looked and it was Jack.

Jack was astonished to see Clara. She seemed like a fairy descended from the sky, he thought to himself.

Jack extended his hand towards Clara and said, "Here, take this small token of love, a bouquet of roses for you." Clara was overjoyed and excited. She accepted it. Then Jack said, "Come, sit here."

As Clara approached the table, Jack pulled out a chair for her to sit. Jack was mesmerized, as if he had gotten lost in her eyes. He seemed like he was crazy in love.

Clara didn't understand what was happening, she was feeling very shy.
Jack said to her, "Clara baby, look at me. Give me your beautiful eyes." Clara blushed and looked at him. Clara asked Jack, "What are you looking at like this?"

Jack said, "I am looking at the most beautiful fairy; in my life, I have never seen such a beautiful fairy before. And today, I can't believe that you are sitting in front of me."

Jack was very confused about whether this was true or not. Clara was just smiling in her heart. Jack whistled and signaled the waiter over. He had planned so well that when the waiter arrived, he had a plate decorated with flowers in his hand, and on it was the gift he had prepared for her. Jack told the waiter to leave it there and then he left from there.

Clara said, "Was all this necessary?

You came all this way for me, that was enough." Jack replied, "If I had the whole world, I would still lay it at your feet, and it wouldn't be enough..."

Upon hearing this, Clara felt extremely touched. Jack came closer and put the necklace on her, and Clara replied with a heartfelt "thank you, thank you so much." She then mentioned that she also brought something for him. Jack became excited to know what it was.

Then Clara told Jack to extend his hand forward. He did, and she put the watch on him.

Jack was so overwhelmed with happiness; he felt like he had received the most precious thing in the world.

He said, "Thank you for these beautiful gifts. They will always remain close to my heart…"

Clara asked, “Did you really like the gift that much?”.

He replied, "You can't even imagine how much I liked your gift."

“I feel fortunate that I have received your gift...!!”

Clara said that the watch suits you well.

Jack, holding Clara's hand in his own, asked, 'Would you like to spend the rest of your life with me? Will you give me the right to rule over your heart?'

Clara, smiling softly, replied in a gentle voice, 'Yes, I want to spend my whole life with you,' and said, 'Yes, you have won my heart, from now on, you have the right to this heart and me alone.'
"Jack felt very happy upon hearing Clara's words; his restless heart found peace. Jack asked Clara to share something about herself. She replied, 'My education isn't complete yet, and I prefer simple things.' Clara then asked Jack the same question. He responded similarly, 'I'm still pursuing my education, and I prefer complexity."

Clara replied, "Oh, good," when Jack extended his hand and asked if she would like to dance with him. She replied eagerly, "Sure." They both got busy dancing to the soft sound of the piano playing in the background, wrapping their arms around each other as they danced. That moment became incredibly memorable for both of them.

Clara had never imagined that she would receive such princess treatment.

She had only heard in stories about a princess being loved by a prince and experiencing magical things that seemed impossible. But here, Clara was experiencing it all firsthand. She began to see herself as a princess.

Some time passed in this manner, Now it was time for lunch.

Jack called the waiter by clapping; all the arrangements had already been made.

Jack served with his own hands.

Clara was surprised; all her favorite dishes were there.

She asked, "How do you know so much about me?"

Jack replied, "I've already learned everything about your likes and dislikes… I'll try to do everything according to your preferences."

Now, both of them had lunch together. After a while, Now it was time to leave, Suddenly, both of them became very sad.

Now both of them have left for their respective homes. Jack started to ponder how sweet the fruit of patience is. Today, he realized the effort he had put in to find Clara.
It felt as if his heart was bursting with joy at the thought of meeting her. He was very happy about the meeting with Clara.

Clara was becoming restless, worried about Jack. She spent quite some time in her anxiety, after all, concern is inevitable in love. Until she received any news from Jack, this was her state. Meanwhile, Jack was also troubled, but for a different reason. He was worried because now he was thinking about when he would meet Clara again.

After some time, Jack suddenly messaged, "My love, I have safely reached home, now you can relax." A big smile appeared on Clara's face. Clara had been waiting eagerly for his call.

She was still thinking about Jack when suddenly the phone rang;
Tring Tring~~…

It was his call. Clara picked up the phone with a loving tone and said, "Yes?" Jack asked, "You were thinking about me? Right?"

Clara, surprised, replied, "No, why would I think about you?" Jack said, "Beautiful girls are caught lying quickly.

Clara said, "You're really good at flirting." And then she laughed, with a bit of force in her voice," hahaha…

"Jack replied, "Now everything I say seems like flirting to you, so be it then." Just then, Clara's mom called her. Clara said, "We're busy right now, we'll talk later."

Hearing this, Jack asked her to talk for a bit longer. Clara replied, "No, not right now, I'm busy," saying this affectionately, she hung up the phone.

Jack was on cloud nine today; what was once impossible had become possible. He was dancing with joy. Remembering the moment, he was becoming happy. The sound of his happiness could be heard outside his room.

Suddenly, there was a knock on the door. "Jack, are you fine, dear?" Jack became suddenly silent, and the room fell quiet as if a hush had fallen over it. He said, "Yes, Mom, I'm fine.

So his mom asked, "Son, what's with the noise coming from your room then?"

Jack, with a nervous tone, replied, "Nn.. no, Mom, everything is fine, I was just practicing for the skit for the event." His mom said, "Okay, make sure to focus."

Clara was also feeling a similar way; she began to live with great cheerfulness. As she looked at Jack's gift, a lovely smile appeared on her face. She thought, "I should share all this with Lily."

Clara was contemplating calling her friend when her mom entered her room and said, "Dear, I'm going out to get some household items. It might take me a while. You go ahead and have your meal." Clara replied to her mom, "Okay, Mom. Take care." (Her mom then left.)

She first picked up her phone and called Lily.

The first time, Lily didn't pick up the call.

She tried calling again.

The second time, Lily answered the call and said, "Hello, Clara..!"

Clara said, "Hey, if you're free, please come over to my place. We can chat for a bit and then go shopping."

Lily replied, "Okay, sure. I'll come over."
" I'll be there in just 15-20 minutes, so be ready," Lily said.

Clara responded, "Yeah, okay, that works.
Bye-bye..." and hung up the phone.

Now Lily got ready to go there. She did her makeup nicely. By then, Clara was also getting ready. After a while, Lily reached Clara's house. Clara was sitting in her home's lawn, reading magazines.

But Jack was the only thing on her mind.

When the doorbell rang, Clara snapped out of her thoughts as if she was pulled back to reality. She went and opened the door. Lily greeted her, saying, "Hey, my princess... How are you?" Clara shyly replied, "I'm fine." Lily remarked, "Just fine or absolutely fine?" Clara began to smile softly. So Lily said, "There's something, you seem to be radiating a different kind of joy today...!"

Clara said, "Let me tell you everything. First, let's go shopping, then I'll tell you." Lily replied, "Hurry up, I can't wait anymore." Clara said, "Yes, I'll tell you everything. Don't worry." Saying this, they both locked the doors and set off for shopping. Now they were on the way. Now Lily began to ask, "Come on, tell me what's going on. Why do you seem different today?"

Clara replied, "Listen, I've accepted Jack." Shocked, Lily exclaimed, "What?!" Clara explained, "Yes, I've started to develop feelings for Jack. I've thought a lot about him, and finally, I've made the decision to spend my life with Jack." Lily, with a voice full of surprise, asked, "Are you sure? Are you telling the truth?" Clara lovingly replied, "I'm absolutely sure!" Lily became very happy upon hearing the news. She began saying, "I am so happy for you. I've been telling you for so long to accept her, because in today's world, who waits so long for someone?" Clara replied, "Hmm, you're right." Lily, dancing and jumping with joy, said, "Now it's your turn to treat me today." Clara responded, "Of course, why not?"

So they both went to a nice shopping center, bought dresses, and bought many things. Now when they both came out of the mall, Clara said, "Let's grab something to eat," and they went to have lunch. They went to a good and big restaurant, ordered many dishes, and were waiting. Clara said, "We had met in such a simple cafe; there were so many surprises for me there."

Lily became excited and started listening intently. Clara mentioned that it was very nice to meet. As they conversed, their food was served. They both enjoyed their meal, ordered juices afterward, They took many photos, capturing memories, and enjoyed themselves thoroughly.

Clara received a call from her mom who asked, "Where are you, dear? Have you eaten or not till yet, Clara?"

Clara replied, "Mom, I went for the shopping with Lily, and we've already had lunch. We'll be home in a little while."

Her mother said okay come soon.

With that, she ended the call.

Clara then said to Lily, "Shall we head home now? It's getting quite late." Lily responded, "Yes, let's go; my family must be waiting for me as well." So, they both left to go home

Both of them seemed very happy,
They both reached their respective homes. Clara's mother asked, "How was your day, dear? Did you enjoy?" Clara replied, "Yes, it was fine.

And for you, I've brought a gift." Her mother got excited and asked, "Tell me, what's my gift?" Upon hearing this, Clara happily handed over the gift she had bought from the shopping center.

Her mother asked, "What is this, dear?" Clara simply said, "It's just for you."
Her mother asked why she seemed so happy today. Clara, suddenly shocked, began to think about what to say.

She hesitated and said, "No, Mom, it's nothing."

So Clara's mother asked, "Why do you seem so happy today?" Clara said, "Well, Lily and I went somewhere after a long time, and that's why I feel much better."

Clara's mother said, "That's good. Now, let me open this gift and see." As soon as she opened the gift, it was a lovely dress. She immediately went to the changing room to try it on. She looked very pretty in the dress and was very happy.

A little while later, Clara heard the beep of a message on her phone. She saw it was from Jack, asking if he could call because he missed her a lot. Clara replied with a gentle smile, saying yes, he could call. Jack had been eagerly awaiting Clara's response, so as soon as he saw it, he dialed her number. Clara asked if he had his cellphone in hand, and Jack replied, saying he sometimes patiently waits for her messages and calls, and sometimes impatiently.

Upon hearing this, Clara felt relieved. They continued talking for quite a while, passing the time. Both were focused on advancing in their respective careers, serving as support systems for each other, motivating one another. Before they knew it, Clara's exams were approaching, and she started feeling anxious about how she would manage to clear them. The fear made her feel overwhelmed, forgetting that there was someone who gave her courage, someone who supported her.

Just then, Jack called, and Clara, with a sense of gloom, answered the phone and started talking slowly. Jack understood that something was bothering her as Clara is never upset like this. So, when he asked about the reason for her sadness, he found out about the upcoming exams and lack of preparation.
Hearing this, Jack empathized, saying exams had disheartened his love, and he kept on trying to understand her mood, make her feel better, and motivate her.

Jack kept helping her, and Clara, motivated by his words, started studying. She eventually fell asleep while studying, but Jack stayed awake, listening to her call until she woke up.

Suddenly, Clara's eyes opened, and she saw that Jack hadn't slept, waiting for her to wake up. Seeing this, Clara felt overwhelmingly happy and apologized for making him wait because her eyes had grown heavy, forcing her to sleep.

With a smile, Jack said, "I've never felt this much peace before, and perhaps, this peace is even more comforting than the peace of sleep."

Jack said, "Come on, freshen up and get back to studying. We have exams coming up."

With that, both got busy with their respective tasks. Clara was struggling, but eventually, she became fully prepared. Jack's hard work was paying off, and as the exam time approached, Clara entered the classroom feeling even more nervous.

Jack was quite tense about Clara's studies.

As the exams began, Clara felt a sense of joy because Jack had helped her, and she was well-prepared. She passed each exam with happiness. After finishing her exams, Clara called Jack to thank him, saying that because of him, difficult situations now seemed easier.

Jack lovingly replied, "Give yourself the credit because you had the courage, which is why you cracked the exam. You have the passion to achieve." Clara thanked Jack wholeheartedly.

Time passed, and they continued supporting each other, growing closer. One day, Clara asked Jack if he would be angry if she shared something about her past. Jack laughed and reassured her, saying he wouldn't be upset at all and that their relationship was based on openness.

Clara hesitantly admitted that she had kept something hidden: she used to like someone before but had never told anyone. They were friends, but she had feelings for him. Jack was a bit surprised but responded lovingly, telling her it was okay and that many people have crushes, and it's normal.

Clara felt dejected, but Jack comforted her, saying it was his own foolishness for not being in her life earlier, as if he had been, she wouldn't have liked anyone else.

This made Clara smile slightly, and she jokingly said that he was just trying to make her feel better, but Jack insisted it was the truth, even if it was bitter.

Jack and Clara were happy as they both passed their exams with good grades. Jack thought it would be a good idea to tell their parents about their relationship, but Clara disagreed, fearing their parents' disapproval. Jack insisted, causing an argument.

Amidst their fight, they both concealed their fear of losing each other. Jack tried to explain that telling their parents was important to ensure they stayed together, while Clara feared their parents would separate them if they found out. They were both at a loss about what to do next.

After contemplating the matter for quite some time, they ultimately decided to go ahead and inform their parents about their relationship, with the resolve to convince them if they disagreed.
A few days later, Clara decided to muster the courage to tell her mom about her relationship, hoping to convince her. When she went to her mom, she found her busy cooking.

Her mom asked if everything was okay, sensing Clara's hesitation. Clara was afraid to share with her mom and remained silent.

Her mom noticed her reluctance and commented on her recent change in demeanor, which made Clara even more nervous.

Clara quickly brushed it off, saying she wasn't feeling well. Her mom suggested consulting a doctor, but Clara insisted on resting instead. Changing the topic, Clara retreated to her room.

After entering the room, Clara decided that she had to muster up the courage to tell her mom today. So, she called Lily and discussed the matter with her.

Lily reassured Clara, saying she would stand by her in every situation.

Hearing this, Clara's heart swelled with gratitude, and she told Lily, "I won't find a friend like you even if I search with a lamp."

Lily laughed and said, "Enough of my praise, now go talk to your mom, and if you need me, call me when you feel ready." They hung up, and Clara gathered her courage once again and went to her mom.

She told her mom that she wanted to share something important, and her mom asked if she was feeling unwell.

Clara replied that she wasn't, and her mom asked what was wrong.

Clara then said that she wanted to marry someone she loves. Hearing this, Clara's mom looked at her angrily and asked, "What? You've started liking someone?" She was very angry.

Clara, with a trembling voice and lowered her eyes, replied, "Yes, Mom." Her mom asked, "Who is he?"

Clara narrated everything to her mom. After a moment of silence, Clara's mom erupted in anger, scolding her harshly.

She grabbed Clara's hand and took her to another room. Clara was sobbing heavily, and her mom, in her current anger, threatened to tell everything to Clara's dad, who was out of town and busy with work. They didn't talk much because of his busy schedule.

Clara cried even harder upon hearing this. Her mom took away her cell phone, scolded her severely, and Clara kept pleading through her tears, "No, Mom, don't treat me like this. Please forgive me."

Then, Clara's mom said loudly, "I will never let you marry him. You will never speak to Jack. I won't allow it."

Hearing this, Clara cried even more, saying, "No, Mom, I will die without him. I love him so much. My life is nothing without him."

Clara's mom, trying to reason, said, "He's not perfect for you; you won't be happy with him." Clara sobbed and replied, "I'll be happy with him. Please, Mom, don't keep me away from Jack. Please, Mom."

Seeing Clara cry so much, her mom calmed down a bit.

Her understanding began to open up.

Clara's mother took a deep breath and said, "Okay, we'll look into it first and then make a decision. I can't say anything right now; but since you are insisting, we will consider it."

Clara, crying, replied, "Yes, Mom, please, just look into it once. I'll accept whatever decision you make." Clara's mother comforted her and handed her cell phone back. Clara thanked her mother with a smile. Her mother then said, "Now go to your room and focus on your studies."

Hearing this, Clara said, "Okay, Mom," and wiping her tears, she went to her room. She immediately called Jack. When Jack answered, he said, "Hello, Clara, how are you?"
Clara, still sounding very upset, said, "I'm fine." Hearing her voice, Jack was surprised and asked, "What's wrong, my doll? Why are you crying?" Then Clara told Jack everything.

Jack listened to everything Clara said and responded with just one thing, "Be patient, my love. Everything will be alright, don't worry. Just let things continue as they are for a few more days."

Clara softly replied, "Okay, I will do everything to be with you."
Just then, Jack's mom called him and got him busy with some chores. Both Jack and Clara got occupied with their respective tasks.

Days passed in this manner. One day, Clara randomly called Jack, but he had gone horse riding and left his phone on the desk.

The phone started ringing, "Tring~tring, tring~tring."

Jack's mom, who was nearby, noticed the ringing phone. She went to answer it. Clara, thinking it was Jack, said, "Hello dear, where are you?" Jack's mom was shocked and asked, "Who are you?" .

Clara got nervous and stayed silent. Jack's mom repeated, "Who are you, dear?"

Clara replied, "I'm Clara, Jack's friend."

Jack's mom then said, "Jack isn't here right now, he's out. I'll ask him to call you back when he returns." Hearing this, Clara quickly hung up.

Jack's mom was left wondering who this friend was since Jack had never mentioned her. She decided to ask Jack about it. As soon as Jack came home, his mom called him and said she needed to talk to him.

Jack thought his mom needed help with something, so he said, "Yes, Mom, what is it?" She looked at him and asked, "Who is Clara?" Jack was taken aback and wondered what to say.

He replied, "Why, Mom? What happened?" His mom insisted, "Tell me who Clara is. I've never heard of her before." Nervously and hesitantly, he said, "She's my friend..." His mom became suspicious and asked, "A friend or something more?".

In a gentle tone, Jack admitted, "I like her and I want to marry her with your and Dad's approval."

His mom then asked, "Who is she? What is she like? What is her background?" Jack explained everything about Clara in detail. After listening to him, his mom said, "Alright, we'll see."

After this conversation, Jack went to his room and messaged Clara, asking, "Can I call you, sweetheart?"

Clara was having lunch when she saw Jack's message. She replied, "I'll call you back later; I'm having lunch with my mom."

A little while later, when Clara was free, she took the opportunity to call Jack. Jack told her that his mom had asked about her. Clara explained, "Yes, I had called earlier and your mom answered. I got scared and told her I was your friend." Jack reassured her, saying, "Don't stress, everything will be fine."

That same day, Clara received her exam results. Her friend Lily called to inform her that the results were out. Clara was very nervous about checking them. When she finally saw her results, she found out she had passed with first-class honors.

She was overjoyed, her happiness reaching the sky.

The first person she shared this exciting news with was Jack, through a message, and then she told her mom. Her mom was very happy and took Clara out for a celebratory dinner at a nice restaurant.

It was a wonderful day for both of them.

The next day, Clara received a call from her dad, informing her that he was coming home. Clara was thrilled to hear this news and eagerly awaited her dad's arrival.

It was evening, and it was raining heavily. The doorbell rang, and Clara's mom went to open the door. As she opened it, she saw that Clara's dad had arrived. He called out to Clara. When Clara saw him, she ran to him and hugged him. Her dad lovingly patted her head and had brought many gifts for her.

After dinner, everyone went to their rooms to sleep. At that time, Clara's mother told Clara's father everything about Clara's relationship. After listening to everything, he simply said that if he is destined for Clara, then he will be the one. We will learn all the details and then make a decision.

Clara's birthday was on October 26th, and she was eagerly waiting for everyone's wishes.

As soon as the clock struck 12, she received a message on her phone saying, "Happiest birthday, my princess."

Seeing this, Clara was overjoyed, as if she had received the world's greatest treasure. Then her mom and dad came with a cake to surprise her and said, "Happiest birthday, my doll."

Witnessing all this, she was very happy. Both Clara and Jack felt an immense sense of peace. After all this, she fell asleep while reading a book.

The next morning, as usual, Clara's phone beeped with a message: "Good morning, darling! Wake up."

Rubbing her eyes and with a slight smile on her lips, Clara read Jack's message. The message said there was a surprise for her and to get ready quickly and come to Season's Cafe.

Seeing this message, Clara was over the moon with happiness. She replied, "What? A surprise for me?" Jack responded, "Yes, there's a surprise for you. Hurry up and get ready; I'm waiting for you."

Hearing this, Clara quickly got up and got ready. By then, her mother came and asked where she was going.
Clara replied, "Just going out for some work, mom." Her mother suggested she at least have breakfast before leaving, but Clara said, "No, mom, I'm getting late. Bye," and left.

At the cafe, Clara called Jack saying, "I’m here now. Where are you?" Jack told her to come to the first floor where he was waiting.

As soon as she reached there, she saw that the entire floor was decorated. Balloons burst at her entrance, candles were blown, and Jack loudly exclaimed, "Happy birthday to you, my love."

Seeing this, Clara was so overwhelmed with happiness that she went completely blank, unable to comprehend anything. Jack said there was more to the surprise and blew a whistle, which brought out a large cake before her. She was utterly astonished. Jack urged her to cut the cake.

Clara cut the cake and fed a piece to Jack. Jack had brought many gifts for her and gave them to her.

They spent some precious time together, which was very special for both of them. Afterward, they had lunch together.

As it came time to go home, they both became upset. With teary eyes, Jack said they had to leave since it was getting late. Clara said she didn't want to go home and be away from him.

She thanked him profusely for making her day so memorable and her birthday so special, expressing her love for him.

Jack replied that she deserved even more and said, "I love you to the moon and back." Then they both headed home.

After returning home, some time passed, and they grew even closer, their relationship being a mix of sweet and sour moments.

Sometimes they fought, and other times they cried for each other, but they had become very close.

One day, Clara received a message from Jack saying he had good news for her. Excitedly, Clara asked what it was. Jack told her that his results had come out, and he had passed with excellent marks. Moreover, his uncle had brought a great job offer for him. Hearing this, Clara's happiness knew no bounds. They were both overjoyed and began to think that their goal was now within reach. Jack shared all the details about the job with Clara.

Clara listened to everything and wished Jack well for his future. A few days later, on the day of Jack's interview, Clara called him early in the morning to wake him up and gave him good guidance for the interview. Jack freshened up and got ready for his interview.

Meanwhile, Clara was praying for him.

After some time, Jack came out of the interview hall and texted Clara, saying that he had just finished his interview and had been asked to wait for a while for the results.

Clara told him to take care and keep her updated.

After a while, the interviewer called Jack back into the hall and told him to keep working hard as he had been selected for the job.

Hearing this, Jack's eyes filled with tears. He became very emotional and was overwhelmed with joy.

He immediately informed Clara and his mother. Clara, too, had tears of happiness in her eyes. She first thanked God and then shared the news with her mother.

After some time, once everything settled down and Jack was well-adjusted, he decided that he wanted to propose to Clara. He asked his mother to speak to Clara's father on their behalf. Clara's mother agreed, saying she would talk to him after a few days.

However, Jack was not liked by Clara's family; they were not genuinely supportive of the marriage. They began to pressure Clara, and as the days passed, the tension increased.

One day, a major incident occurred: Clara's parents suddenly refused Jack's proposal. Clara was shocked and asked why they had changed their minds when they had previously agreed. Her parents told her they believed they could find a better match for her. Clara, in tears, insisted that she only wanted to marry Jack. She pleaded with them, crying and being very stubborn about her decision.

Seeing Clara so distressed, her parents eventually gave in, realizing she wouldn't listen to any alternatives.

They agreed to the marriage, and Clara finally calmed down. She then informed Jack about everything that had happened and told him that her parents had agreed. She asked him to bring his mother to meet her father.

The very next day, Jack and his mother went to Clara's house. Clara's parents warmly welcomed them. Clara's parents liked Jack, and Jack's mother was very fond of Clara.

The families formally agreed to the marriage and even set a wedding date.
At last, Jack and Clara's dreams were coming true. They had envisioned many dreams together, and now they could see them being realized.

The long-awaited wedding day of Clara and Jack has finally arrived. It marks the culmination of their journey together, filled with love, anticipation, and meticulous planning.

The atmosphere is charged with excitement and joy as friends and family gather to witness the union of two souls, celebrating this significant milestone in their lives.

The ceremony promises to be a beautiful blend of tradition and personal touches, reflecting the couple's unique story and deep commitment to each other.

This day, so eagerly anticipated, will undoubtedly be etched in their hearts forever as they embark on a new chapter together.

And they embark on their journey together, bound by love and commitment, their lives intertwined with hues of devotion and companionship. Sharing every moment, every struggle, and every triumph, their love and dedication keep them united through every twist and turn of life.

Thus, their story remains filled with joy and bliss for all eternity.

Love And Lavender

Poem

"Dreamer's Love"

In a world where dreams take flight,
There lived a girl with eyes so bright,
She danced through realms of fantasy,
With dreams as vast as the endless sea.

Each night she soared on wings of hope,
Through starlit skies where dreams elope,
But in the midst of her endless flight,
She found herself drawn to the soft moonlight.

For there, amidst the shadows deep,
She met a love she could not keep,
A soul whose light matched her own,
A love so pure, like a melody's tone.

Their hearts entwined in sweet embrace,
Two dreamers lost in time and space,
Together they danced in the realm of dreams,
Where reality fades and nothing's as it seems.

But as the dawn broke, their love did wane,
For dreams, like shadows, cannot remain,
And though they parted, their love did bloom,
In the heart of the dreamer, amidst the gloom.

For in the end, it was not the dream they sought,
But the love they found, the battles they fought,
And though they may wander worlds apart,
Their love lives on, a flame in the heart.

So here's to the dreamers, who dare to believe,
In love that transcends, in dreams that deceive,
For in the end, it's the love we hold dear,
That makes life worth living, that conquers our fear….

For you....

In your eyes, I find solace amidst life's chaos, and in your embrace, I discover the true meaning of home. Every heartbeat echoes the symphony of our love, a melody composed of whispered promises and shared dreams. With you, each moment is a canvas painted with the hues of passion and affection, weaving a tapestry of endless devotion. Forever entwined, our souls dance to the rhythm of a love story written in the stars, destined to shine brighter with each passing day.

Though miles may separate us, our love knows no bounds. Across the vast expanse of distance, my heart beats only for you, bridging the gap with every thought of your smile and every whispered "I love you." In the silence of night, I find solace knowing that our love transcends space and time, binding us together even when apart. With each passing day, our connection grows stronger, fueled by the unwavering commitment we share. Until the day we are reunited, my love for you remains steadfast and true, a beacon of hope guiding us through the distance until we're finally together again..

Echoes of Love

Story

In the quaint town of Willowbrook, where the sun-kissed meadows met the whispering woods, there existed a tale as old as time itself - a tale of love transcending barriers, echoing through generations. At the heart of this narrative were two souls, Eleanor and James, whose fates intertwined amidst the blooming cherry blossoms of spring.

Eleanor, with her luminous hazel eyes and a smile that could melt even the coldest of hearts, was the daughter of the town's esteemed florist. Her days were spent amidst the fragrant blooms, tending to the flowers with the same tenderness she held in her heart.

James, on the other hand, was a wanderer, a troubadour whose melodies echoed through the cobbled streets of Willowbrook. With his guitar as his only companion, he wandered from town to town, weaving tales of love and longing with every strum of his strings.

It was on a balmy afternoon, beneath the swaying branches of an ancient oak tree, that Eleanor first laid eyes on James. His fingers danced effortlessly across the strings of his guitar, his voice carrying melodies that stirred something deep within her soul. From that moment on, she found herself drawn to him, like a moth to a flame.

Their encounters were fleeting at first, mere glimpses exchanged in the bustling marketplace or stolen moments by the riverside. Yet with each passing day, their connection grew stronger, blossoming into a love that defied all logic and reason.

But theirs was not a love without obstacles. For Eleanor belonged to a family of high standing, while James was but a humble minstrel with dreams that reached far beyond the confines of Willowbrook. Society frowned upon their union, deeming it an abomination of class and status.

Despite the whispers and the disapproving glances, Eleanor and James remained steadfast in their love, their hearts beating as one against the tide of adversity. Together, they found solace in the beauty of their shared moments, cherishing each stolen kiss and whispered promise as if it were their last.

Yet fate, with its cruel sense of irony, had other plans in store for them. On the eve of their secret elopement, tragedy struck the town of Willowbrook, casting a shadow of despair upon its unsuspecting inhabitants. A devastating storm ravaged the countryside, leaving behind a trail of destruction in its wake.

In the chaos that ensued, Eleanor and James were torn apart, their hopes of a future together shattered like fragile glass. With the rivers overflowing and the bridges collapsing, they found themselves on opposite sides of a chasm too wide to traverse.

For days on end, Eleanor searched tirelessly for her beloved, her heart heavy with grief and longing. Yet no matter how far she wandered or how loud she called out his name, James remained but a distant echo, a memory fading with each passing day.

Months turned into years, and still, Eleanor refused to give up hope. She tended to her flowers with a quiet determination, her spirit unbroken despite the ache in her heart. And then, one fateful day, as the cherry blossoms bloomed once more, fate intervened in the most unexpected of ways.

It was a warm spring morning when a weary traveler stumbled upon the town of Willowbrook, his clothes tattered and his spirit broken. With each step he took, he felt as though he were walking through a haze, his mind clouded with memories of a love lost to the ages.

But as he wandered through the familiar streets, something stirred within him, a faint whisper of recognition that tugged at his heartstrings. And then, like a bolt of lightning illuminating the darkest of nights, he saw her - Eleanor, the woman he had loved with every fiber of his being.

With tears streaming down her cheeks, Eleanor rushed into his arms, her laughter mingling with his own as they embraced beneath the blooming cherry blossoms. In that moment, all the pain and sorrow of their past melted away, leaving nothing but the purest of love in its wake. And so, against all odds, Eleanor and James found their way back to each other, their love stronger than ever before. For theirs was a love that transcended time and space, echoing through the ages like a timeless melody, forever etched in the annals of history.

Vengeance of the Heart

Story

In the labyrinthine streets of the ancient city of Verona, where whispered secrets mingled with the scent of betrayal, there existed a tale of love and revenge that echoed through the cobblestone alleys. At the heart of this narrative were two souls, Isabella and Lorenzo, whose destinies became entwined amidst the tumultuous currents of passion and deception.

Isabella, with her fiery spirit and bewitching allure, was the daughter of the city's most prominent nobleman. Her beauty was legendary, her laughter like music to the ears of those who were fortunate enough to bask in its radiance. Yet beneath her facade of elegance lay a heart hardened by the sting of betrayal, a heart yearning for justice and retribution.

Lorenzo, on the other hand, was a man of humble origins, a blacksmith's apprentice whose hands were calloused from years of toil at the forge. Despite his lowly station in life, he possessed a charm and charisma that drew others to him like moths to a flame. But beneath his rugged exterior lay a burning desire for vengeance, a desire fueled by the injustices he had suffered at the hands of the aristocracy.

Their paths first crossed on a moonlit night, beneath the shadow of the ancient oak tree that stood sentinel over the city. Isabella, disguised in a cloak of midnight velvet, had ventured out into the darkness in search of solace from the turmoil that plagued her mind. And there, amidst the whispering leaves and the haunting melody of the nightingale, she stumbled upon Lorenzo, his eyes ablaze with a fire that mirrored her own.

From that moment on, their fates became intertwined, their destinies bound by a love that burned with the intensity of a thousand suns. Yet theirs was not a love without obstacles, for Isabella was betrothed to another, a cruel and calculating nobleman who sought to possess her as he would a prized possession.

But Isabella's heart belonged to Lorenzo, and she vowed to defy convention and tradition in order to be with him. Together, they embarked on a clandestine affair, stealing moments of passion and stolen kisses beneath the cloak of darkness. Yet their forbidden love did not go unnoticed, and soon, whispers of scandal and betrayal began to spread like wildfire through the city streets.

Enraged by Isabella's defiance, her betrothed vowed to destroy the object of her affection, to crush him beneath the heel of his polished boot like an insignificant insect. And so, with the cunning of a fox and the cruelty of a viper, he set in motion a plan that would bring about the downfall of both Isabella and Lorenzo.

Under the cover of darkness, Isabella was lured into a trap, her innocence and virtue called into question by those who sought to tarnish her reputation. Accused of treason and infidelity, she was cast out from her father's house, her name dragged through the mud by those who reveled in her downfall.

Heartbroken and destitute, Isabella turned to Lorenzo for solace, only to find that he too had fallen victim to her betrothed's machinations. Framed for a crime he did not commit, Lorenzo was thrown into the dungeons beneath the city, his spirit broken and his hope all but extinguished.

But even in the darkest of times, love has a way of persevering, of shining like a beacon in the blackest of nights. And so it was that Isabella vowed to seek vengeance upon those who had wronged them, to reclaim their honor and their dignity at any cost.

Armed with nothing but her wits and her indomitable spirit, Isabella embarked on a journey of revenge, weaving a web of deceit and intrigue that ensnared her enemies like flies in a spider's trap. With each calculated move, she drew closer to her ultimate goal, her heart consumed by a burning desire for justice.

And then, on a fateful night bathed in the glow of the full moon, Isabella's moment of reckoning arrived. With the precision of a master strategist, she orchestrated a daring rescue mission, freeing Lorenzo from his prison cell and leading him to safety beneath the cover of darkness.

Together, they fled into the night, their hearts pounding with the exhilaration of freedom and the promise of a new beginning. And as they disappeared into the shadows, leaving behind the city that had once been their home, they vowed to never look back, to forge a new destiny together far from the reach of those who sought to destroy them.

For theirs was a love born of adversity, a love that had weathered the storm of betrayal and emerged stronger and more resilient than ever before. And as they rode off into the unknown, hand in hand and heart in heart, they knew that no matter what trials lay ahead, they would face them together, united in their shared quest for love and revenge.

Whispers of Willow Creek

Story

In the quiet town of Willow Creek, where whispers danced on the misty nights, Lily closed the library, her mind alive with the tales of mystery she had just shelved. As she walked home, the fog thickened around her, and in its midst stood a figure by the ancient oak. His presence, shrouded in mystery, intrigued her.

"Hello," Lily called, her voice barely reaching the stranger.

He turned, revealing piercing blue eyes that seemed to hold secrets untold. "I'm Ethan," he said, his voice smooth like silk.

Lily's curiosity piqued. "Lily," she replied, stepping closer.

Ethan explained his quest for inspiration, and Lily, sensing a kindred spirit, invited him to stay at her guesthouse. Together, they walked through the fog, their conversation weaving tales of the past and dreams of the future.

As days turned into nights, Ethan's presence brought a new energy to Willow Creek. He and Lily explored the town, uncovering its hidden nooks and crannies, and delving into the stories of its inhabitants.

But beneath the surface of tranquility, whispers lingered in the mist, hinting at secrets long forgotten. Lily and Ethan found themselves drawn into the enigma of Willow Creek, their hearts entwined in both romance and mystery.

Together, they unearthed fragments of the town's past—a tragic love story, a buried treasure, and a curse that had plagued Willow Creek for generations. As they pieced together the puzzle, they realized that their fates were intertwined with those who had come before them.

But as they delved deeper, they awakened forces beyond their control. Dark shadows crept through the fog, threatening to tear apart the fragile peace they had found.

In the midst of chaos, Lily and Ethan clung to each other, their love a beacon of light in the darkness. With courage and determination, they confronted the malevolent spirit that lurked in the mist, unraveling its grip on the town.

In a final showdown, Lily and Ethan faced the source of Willow Creek's torment—a vengeful soul trapped between worlds. With the power of their love, they banished the spirit, freeing Willow Creek from its curse.

As the fog lifted, revealing the dawn of a new day, Lily and Ethan stood hand in hand, their hearts full of hope. Together, they had conquered the mysteries of Willow Creek, forging a bond that would endure for eternity.

Acknowludgement

The creation of this book has been a journey marked by profound gratitude and unwavering support from my family, friends and specially from my sister. Their encouragement, wisdom, and unwavering commitment have shaped this work in profound ways.

I am deeply indebted to Mom and dad, whose guidance and encouragement have been indispensable throughout every phase of this endeavor. Their insights and unwavering belief in this project have been a constant source of inspiration.

Gratitude extends to "AL-LINA publications" for their invaluable resources and support, which have enriched the fabric of this book.

Special appreciation goes to MY LOVE, for his exceptional contributions and unwavering dedication to excellence.

We thank the god almighty,
our teachers, students, colleagues
and our family for all the support and motivation.

LOTS OF LOVE FROM

AUTHOR : SHABNAM SIRAJ

PUBLISHER : AL – LINA PUBLICATION

CONTACTS

Gmail : linapublication@gmail.com
Whatsapp : (+91) 7200067595
Instagram : @allina_publication

www.ingramcontent.com/pod-product-compliance
Lightning Source LLC
Chambersburg PA
CBHW022203160726
48282CB00024B/318
9789394702547